# HOW TO LOVE

## THICH NHAT HANH

PARALLAX
PRESS

Berkeley, California

35049 84

Parallax Press
P.O. Box 7355
Berkeley, California 94707
www.parallax.org

Parallax Press is the publishing division of
Unified Buddhist Church, Inc.
© 2015 by Unified Buddhist Church
All rights reserved
Printed in The United States of America

Cover and text design by Debbie Berne
Illustrations by Jason DeAntonis

ISBN: 978-1-937006-88-4

Library of Congress Cataloging-in-Publication Data

Nhat Hanh, Thich, author.
 How to love / Thich Nhat Hanh.
    pages cm
 Includes bibliographical references.
 ISBN 978-1-937006-88-4
1.  Love—Religious aspects—Buddhism. 2.
Buddhism—Spiritual life.  I. Title.
 BQ9800.T5392N45449 2015
 294.3'5677--dc23
                                    2014041483


2 3 4 5 / 18 17 16 15

# CONTENTS

# NOTES ON LOVE

# HEART LIKE A RIVER

If you pour a handful of salt into a cup of water, the water becomes undrinkable. But if you pour the salt into a river, people can continue to draw the water to cook, wash, and drink. The river is immense, and it has the capacity to receive, embrace, and transform. When our hearts are small, our understanding and compassion are limited, and we suffer. We can't accept or tolerate others and their shortcomings, and we demand that they change. But when our hearts expand, these same things don't make us suffer anymore. We have a lot of understanding and compassion and can embrace others. We accept others as they are, and then they have a chance to transform. So the big question is: how do we help our hearts to grow?

## FEEDING OUR LOVE

Each of us can learn the art of nourishing happiness and love. Everything needs food to live, even love. If we don't know how to nourish our love, it withers. When we feed and support our own happiness, we are nourishing our ability to love. That's why to love means to learn the art of nourishing our happiness.

## UNDERSTANDING IS THE NATURE OF LOVE

Understanding someone's suffering is the best gift you can give another person. Understanding is love's other name. If you don't understand, you can't love.

## RECOGNIZING TRUE LOVE

True love gives us beauty, freshness, solidity, freedom, and peace. True love includes a feeling of deep joy that we are alive. If we don't feel this way when we feel love, then it's not true love.

## REVERENCE IS THE NATURE OF OUR LOVE

There's a tradition in Asia of treating your partner with the respect you would accord a guest. This is true even if you have been with your loved one for a long time. The other person always deserves your full respect. Reverence is the nature of our love.

## LOVE IS EXPANSIVE

In the beginning of a relationship, your love may include only you and the other person. But if you practice true love, very soon that love will grow and include all of us. The moment love stops growing, it begins to die. It's like a tree; if a tree stops growing, it begins to die. We can learn how to feed our love and help it continue to grow.

## LOVE IS ORGANIC

Love is a living, breathing thing. There is no
need to force it to grow in a particular direction. If we start by being easy and gentle with
ourselves, we will find it is just there inside of
us, solid and healing.

## DISTRACTIONS

Often, we get crushes on others not because we truly love and understand them, but to distract ourselves from our suffering. When we learn to love and understand ourselves and have true compassion for ourselves, then we can truly love and understand another person.

## THE FOUR ELEMENTS OF TRUE LOVE

True love is made of four elements: loving kindness, compassion, joy, and equanimity. In Sanskrit, these are, *maitri, karuna, mudita,* and *upeksha.* If your love contains these elements, it will be healing and transforming, and it will have the element of holiness in it. True love has the power to heal and transform any situation and bring deep meaning to our lives.

## LOVING KINDNESS

The first element of true love is loving kindness. The essence of loving kindness is being able to offer happiness. You can be the sunshine for another person. You can't offer happiness until you have it for yourself. So build a home inside by accepting yourself and learning to love and heal yourself. Learn how to practice mindfulness in such a way that you can create moments of happiness and joy for your own nourishment. Then you have something to offer the other person.

## COMPASSION

The second element of true love is compassion. Compassion is the capacity to understand the suffering in oneself and in the other person. If you understand your own suffering, you can help him to understand his suffering. Understanding suffering brings compassion and relief. You can transform your own suffering and help transform the suffering of the other person with the practice of mindfulness and looking deeply.

## JOY

The third element of true love is the capacity
to offer joy. When you know how to generate
joy, it nourishes you and nourishes the other
person. Your presence is an offering, like fresh
air, or spring flowers, or the bright blue sky.

# EQUANIMITY

The fourth element of true love is equanimity.
We can also call it inclusivesness or nondiscrimination. In a deep relationship, there's no
longer a boundary between you and the other
person. You are her and she is you. Your suffering is her suffering. Your understanding of
your own suffering helps your loved one to
suffer less. Suffering and happiness are no longer individual matters. What happens to your
loved one happens to you. What happens to
you happens to your loved one.

## RESPECT AND TRUST

Along with the traditional four elements of true love—loving kindness, compassion, joy, and equanimity—there are two more elements: respect and trust. These elements can be found in the four, but it helps to mention their names. When you love someone, you have to have trust and confidence. Love without trust is not yet love. Of course, first you have to have trust, respect, and confidence in yourself. Trust that you have a good and compassionate nature. You are part of the universe; you are made of stars. When you look at your loved one, you see that he is also made of stars and carries eternity inside. Looking in this way, we naturally feel reverence. True love cannot be without trust and respect for oneself and for the other person.

# BE BEAUTIFUL, BE YOURSELF

If you can accept your body, then you have a chance to see your body as your home. You can rest in your body, settle in, relax, and feel joy and ease. If you don't accept your body and your mind, you can't be at home with yourself. You have to accept yourself as you are. This is a very important practice. As you practice building a home in yourself, you become more and more beautiful.

## YOU ARE A FLOWER

Every child is born in the garden of human-
ity as a flower. Each flower differs from every
other flower. There are many messages in our
society that tell us, even when we're young
people, that there's something wrong with us
and that if we just buy the right product, or
look a certain way, or have the right partner,
that will fix it. As grown-ups, we can remind
young people that they're already beautiful as
they are; they don't have to be someone else.

## WATERING THE FLOWER
## IN A FRIEND

One day I was giving a talk at our practice center in France. Two of the people in attendance
were a couple from Bordeaux who visit our
center on occasion. The woman was sitting in
the front of the audience, and she was crying
from the beginning of the talk to the end. After
the talk I went to her husband and told him,
"Dear friend, your flower needs some water."
He understood right away. After lunch, they
drove home through the countryside, and he
spent that hour and a half letting her know all
the things he appreciated about her. When
they arrived home, their children were sur-
prised to see their mother and father so joyful.
Transformation can happen very quickly.

## HUGGING

In 1966, a friend took me to the Atlanta Airport.
When we were saying good-bye she asked,
"Is it all right to hug a Buddhist monk?" In
my country, we're not used to expressing
ourselves that way, but I thought, "I'm a Zen
teacher. It should be no problem for me to do
that." So I said, "Why not?" and she hugged
me, but I was quite stiff. While on the plane, I
decided that if I wanted to work with friends in
the West, I would have to learn the culture of
the West. So I invented hugging meditation.
Hugging meditation is a combination of East
and West. According to the practice, you have
to really hug the person you are holding. You

have to make him or her very real in your arms, not just for the sake of appearances, patting him on the back to pretend you are there, but breathing consciously and hugging with all your body, spirit, and heart. Hugging meditation is a practice of mindfulness. "Breathing in, I know my dear one is in my arms, alive. Breathing out, she is so precious to me." If you breathe deeply like that, holding the person you love, the energy of your care and appreciation will penetrate into that person and she will be nourished and bloom like a flower.

# BODY AND MIND

Body and mind are not two separate entities. What happens in the body will have an effect on the mind and vice versa. Mind relies on the body to manifest, and body relies on mind in order to be alive, in order to be possible. When you love someone, you have to respect her, not only her mind but also her body. You respect your own body, and you respect her body. Your body is you. Your body is your mind. The other person's mind and body are also connected.

## SPIRITUAL PRACTICE

Spirituality doesn't mean a blind belief in a spiritual teaching. Spirituality is a practice that brings relief, communication, and transformation. Everyone needs a spiritual dimension in life. Without a spiritual dimension, it's very challenging to be with the daily difficulties we all encounter. With a spiritual practice, you're no longer afraid. Along with your physical body, you have a spiritual body. The practices of breathing, walking, concentration, and understanding can help you greatly in dealing with your emotions, in listening to and embracing your suffering, and in helping you to recognize and embrace the suffering of another person. If we have this capacity, then we can develop a real and lasting spiritual intimacy with ourselves and with others.

## THREE KINDS OF INTIMACY

There are three kinds of intimacy: physical, emotional, and spiritual. These three should go together. Every one of us is seeking emotional intimacy. We want to have real communication, mutual understanding, and communion. We want to be in harmony with someone. When an intimate relationship contains all three elements, then physical intimacy is more meaningful and can be very healthy and healing.

## EMPTY SEX

Sexual desire is not love. Sexual activity without love is called empty sex. If you satisfy your body but don't satisfy your heart and your mind, are you satisfied? Do you feel whole and connected? When your body, heart, and mind are satisfied, sexual intimacy connects you more deeply with yourself and your partner.

## SAYING "NO"

Loving someone doesn't mean saying "yes" to whatever the other person wants. The basis of loving someone else is to know yourself and to know what you need. I know a woman who suffered very much because she couldn't say "no." From the time she was young, whenever a man asked her for something, she felt she had to say "yes" even when she didn't want to. It's important that loving another person doesn't take priority over listening to yourself and knowing what you need.

## THREE STRONG ROOTS

To keep our commitment to our partner, and to weather the most difficult storms, we need strong roots. If we wait until there is trouble with our partner to try and solve it, we won't have built strong enough roots to withstand the assault. Often we think we're balanced when, in reality, that balance is fragile. We only need a slight breeze to blow for us to fall down. A juniper tree has its roots planted deep in the heart of the earth. As a result it is solid and strong. But some trees that appear to be quite steady, need only one raging storm to knock them down. Resilient trees can weather a violent storm because their roots are deep and firm. The roots of a lasting relationship are mindfulness, deep listening and loving speech, and a strong community to support you.

## SHARING THE
## SAME ASPIRATION

In a relationship, when you and your partner share the same kind of aspiration, you become one, and you become an instrument of love and peace in the world. You begin as a community of two people, and then you can grow your community. In the practice center where I live, there are over a hundred of us. We have the same concerns, the same desires, and the same future. There is no longer a place for jealousy, because we are all faithful to the same aspiration. We share everything, but we still have our freedom intact. Love is not a kind of prison. True love gives us a lot of space.

## LOVING COMMUNICATION

To love without knowing *how* to love wounds the person we love. To know how to love someone, we have to understand them. To understand, we need to listen. That person may be our partner, our friend, our sibling, or our child. You can ask, "Dear one, do you think that I understand you enough? Please tell me your difficulties, your suffering, and your deepest wishes." Then the other person has an opportunity to open their heart.

## BREATHING TO AVOID AN ARGUMENT

Everyone knows that blaming and arguing never help; but we forget. Conscious breathing helps us develop the ability to stop at that crucial moment, to keep ourselves from saying or doing something we regret later. Practice conscious breathing when things are going well with your partner, then it will be there for you when things get hard.

## LISTENING WITH PATIENCE

When your loved one is talking, practice listening deeply. Sometimes the other person will say something that surprises us, that is the opposite of the way we see things. Allow the other person to speak freely. Don't cut your loved one off or criticize their words. When we listen deeply with all our heart—for ten minutes, half an hour, or even an hour—we will begin to see the other person more deeply and understand them better. If they say something that's incorrect, that's based on a wrong perception, we can give them a little information later on to help them correct their thinking. But right now, we just listen.

## LIBERATION FROM COMPLEXES

Often we can't love ourselves or others fully when we're stuck in our own complexes. When you have an inferiority complex, you have low self-esteem, and this is a kind of sickness. High self-esteem is also a sickness, because you consider yourself to be above others and that causes suffering as well. Although equality is something good, it can also be a complex. When you say, "I'm as good as he is," you still think you have a separate self. When you compare two selves to each other, suffering will result. Real liberty is freedom from all these complexes.

## A TRUE PARTNER

We tend to wonder if we have enough to offer
in a relationship. We're thirsty for truth, goodness, compassion, spiritual beauty, so we go
looking outside. Sometimes we think we've
found a partner who embodies all that is good,
beautiful, and true. After a time, we usually
discover that we've had a wrong perception of
that person, and we become disappointed. A
true partner or friend is one who encourages
you to look deep inside yourself for the beauty
and love you've been seeking.

## JOY IS HEALING

If a relationship can't provide joy, then it's
not true love. If you keep making the other
person cry all day, that's not true love. Offer
only the things that can make the other person
happy. You should know the real needs of that
person. Practice and learn how to generate
a feeling of joy, a feeling of happiness with
your in-breath, your out-breath, and your
steps. If you have enough understanding and
love, then every moment—whether it's spent
making breakfast, driving the car, watering the
garden, or doing anything else in your day—
can be a moment of joy.

## NOURISHED BY JOY

Learn to nourish yourself and the other
person with joy. Are you able to make the
other person smile? Are you able to increase
her confidence and enthusiasm? If you're not
able to do these small things for her, how
can you say you love her? Sometimes a kind
word is enough to help someone blossom like
a flower.

## ATTENTION

As long as we're rejecting ourselves and causing harm to our bodies and minds, there's no point in talking about loving and accepting others. With mindfulness, we can recognize our habitual ways of thinking and the contents of our thoughts. Sometimes our thoughts run around in circles and we're engulfed in distrust, pessimism, conflict, sorrow, or jealousy. This state of mind will naturally manifest in our words and actions and cause harm to us and to others. When we shed the light of mindfulness on our habitual thought patterns, we see them clearly. Recognizing our habits and smiling to them is the practice of appropriate mental attention, which helps us create new and more beneficial neural pathways.

## LOVER AS HEALER

The Sanskrit word *karuna* is often translated as "compassion." Compassion means to "suffer with" another person, to share their suffering. Karuna is much more than that. It's the capacity to remove and transform suffering, not just to share it. When you go to a doctor, it doesn't help if she just shares your suffering. A doctor has to help heal the suffering. When you love someone, you should have the capacity to bring relief and help him to suffer less. This is an art. If you don't understand the roots of his suffering, you can't help, just as a doctor can't help heal your illness if she doesn't know the cause. You need to understand the cause of your loved one's suffering in order to help bring relief.

## LOVING MINDFULLY

"Love" is a beautiful word, and we have to restore its meaning. When we say, "I love hamburgers," we spoil the word. We have to make the effort to heal words by using them properly and carefully. True love includes a sense of responsibility and accepting the other person as she is, with all her strengths and weaknesses. If you only like the best things in a person, that is not love. You have to accept her weaknesses and bring your patience, understanding, and energy to help her transform. This kind of love brings protection and safety.

## NONDISCRIMINATION

In true love, there's no more separation or discrimination. His happiness is your happiness. Your suffering is his suffering. You can no longer say, "That's your problem." In true love, both happiness and suffering are no longer individual matters. You are him, and he is you. In a good relationship we are like two fingers of the same hand. The little finger doesn't suffer from an inferiority complex and say, "I'm so small. I wish I were as big as the thumb." The thumb doesn't have a superiority complex, saying, "I'm more important. I'm the big brother of all the fingers; you have to obey me." Instead, there's a perfect collaboration between them.

## ASKING FOR HELP

When you suffer, you may want to go to your room, lock the door, and cry. The person who hurt you is the last person you want to see. Even if he tries to approach you, you may still be very angry. But to get relief, you have to go to the person you love, the one who just hurt you very deeply, and ask for help. Become yourself one hundred percent. Open your mouth and say with all your heart and with all your concentration that you suffer and you need help.

# THREE HELPFUL SENTENCES

It's not healthy to keep anger inside for too long. If you're too upset to speak calmly, you can write a note and put it where the other person will see it. Here are three sentences that may help. First: "My dear, I am suffering, I am angry, and I want you to know it." The second is: "I am doing my best." This means you are practicing mindful breathing and walking, and you are refraining from doing or saying anything out of anger. The third is: "Please help me." Memorize these sentences. Or write them on a small piece of paper, the size of a credit card, and put it in your wallet. Then when you're angry, you can take it out, and you will know exactly what to do.

# ARE YOU SURE?

Other people's actions are the result of their own pain and not the result of any intention to hurt you. A wrong perception can be the cause of a lot of suffering. This is why, whenever we have a perception, we have to ask ourselves if our perception is right. When we stand with friends looking at the setting sun, we're sure the sun has not set quite yet. But a scientist might tell us that the sun we're seeing is only the image of the sun of eight minutes ago. We are subject to thousands of wrong perceptions like this in our daily lives. The next time you suffer, and you believe that your suffering has been caused by the person you love the most, ask your loved one for help.

## PRIDE

Often, our pride stands in the way of our asking for help. In true love there is no place for pride. To love each other means to trust each other. If you don't tell the person you love of your suffering, it means you don't love this person enough to trust her. You have to realize that this person is the best person to help you. We need to be able to get help from the person we love.

## REDISCOVERING APPRECIATION

When a loved one is suffering a lot, he or she doesn't have enough energy to embrace you and help you to suffer less. So it's natural that you become disappointed. You think that the other person's presence is no longer helpful to you. You may even wonder if you love this person anymore. If you're patient and you practice taking care of yourself and the other person, you may have a chance to discover that the elements of goodness and beauty in the person you love are still there. Taking care of yourself, you can support your loved one and reestablish the joy in your relationship.

## A DEEP THIRST

Sometimes we feel empty; we feel a vacuum,
a great lack of something. We don't know
the cause; it's very vague, but that feeling of
being empty inside is very strong. We expect
and hope for something much better so we'll
feel less alone, less empty. The desire to
understand ourselves and to understand life
is a deep thirst. There's also the deep thirst
to be loved and to love. We are ready to love
and be loved. It's very natural. But because
we feel empty, we try to find an object of our
love. Sometimes we haven't had the time to
understand ourselves, yet we've already found
the object of our love. When we realize that all
our hopes and expectations of course can't
be fulfilled by that person, we continue to feel
empty. You want to find something, but you

don't know what to search for. In everyone there's a continuous desire and expectation; deep inside, you still expect something better to happen. That is why you check your email many times a day!

## A POT IN SEARCH OF A LID

Very often we feel like a pot without a lid.
We believe that our lid is somewhere in the
world and that if we look very hard, we'll find
the right lid to cover our pot. The feeling of
emptiness is always there inside us. When we
contemplate the other person, sometimes we
think we see what we feel we lack. We think
we need someone else to lean on, to take ref-
uge in, and to diminish our suffering. We want
to be the object of another person's attention
and contemplation. We want someone who
will look at us and embrace our feeling of emptiness and suffering with his energy of mindfulness. Soon we become addicted to that kind
of energy; we think that without that attention,

we can't live. It helps us feel less empty and helps us forget the block of suffering inside. When we ourselves can't generate the energy to take care of ourselves, we think we need the energy of someone else. We focus on the need and the lack rather than generating the energy of mindfulness, concentration, and insight that can heal our suffering and help the other person as well.

## BEFORE COMMITTING
## TO ANOTHER

There was a couple who were about to get married in Plum Village, the practice center where I live. They wanted to see me before the wedding ceremony and I received them in my hut. They said, "Thay, there are only twenty-four hours left before our wedding. What do you think that we can do to prepare for our married life to be successful?" I said, "The most important thing for you to do is to look deeply into yourself, to see if there is something that is still an obstacle for you. Is there anyone with whom you haven't reconciled? Is there anything within you that you haven't reconciled with?" Reconciliation can also be with your own self. If you don't reconcile with yourself, happiness with another person is impossible.

## RECONCILING FROM A DISTANCE

Even if the person with whom you need to reconcile is very far away, you can still do the work of reconciliation now. What is important is to reconcile within your own heart and mind. If reconciliation is done within, that is enough. Because the effect of that reconciliation will be felt everywhere later on. Even if the person you want to reconcile with refuses to respond, or even if she's already dead, reconciliation is still possible. Reconciliation means to work it out within yourself so that peace can be restored. Reconcile with yourself for the sake of the world, for the sake of all living beings. Your peace and serenity are crucial for all of us.

## STARTING A FAMILY

Before having a child, it would be wonderful if people would take a year to look deeply into themselves, to practice loving speech and deep listening, and to learn the other practices that will help them enjoy themselves and their children more. Bringing a new life into the world is a serious matter. Taking a year for introspection and preparation doesn't seem too much. Doctors and therapists spend up to ten years to get a license. But anyone can become a parent without any training or preparation. Parents can learn how to sow seeds of happiness, peace, and joy in the new child.

## THE PRACTICE OF METTA

To love is, first of all, to accept ourselves as we actually are. The first practice of love is to know oneself. The Pali word *metta* means "loving kindness." When we practice Metta Meditation, we see the conditions that have caused us to be the way we are; this makes it easy for us to accept ourselves, including our suffering and our happiness. When we practice Metta Meditation, we touch our deepest aspirations. But the willingness and aspiration to love is not yet love. We have to look deeply, with all our being, in order to understand the object of our meditation. The practice of love meditation is not autosuggestion. We have to look deeply at our body, feelings, perceptions, mental formations, and consciousness. We can observe how much peace, happiness, and lightness we already have. We can notice whether we are anxious about accidents or misfortunes, and how much anger, irritation, fear, anxiety, or worry are still in us. As we become aware of the feelings in us, our self-understanding will deepen. We will see how our fears and lack of peace contribute to our unhappiness, and we will see the value of loving ourselves and cultivating a heart of compassion. Love will enter our thoughts, words, and actions.

## DIGGING DEEP

Practicing loving kindness meditation is like digging deep into the ground until we reach the purest water. We look deeply into ourselves until insight arises and our love flows to the surface. Joy and happiness radiate from our eyes, and everyone around us benefits from our smile and our presence. If we take good care of ourselves, we help everyone. We stop being a source of suffering to the world, and we become a reservoir of joy and freshness. Here and there are people who know how to take good care of themselves, who live joyfully and happily. They are our strongest support. Whatever they do, they do for everyone.

## MAKING MISTAKES

Since we're human beings, we make mistakes. We cause others to suffer. We hurt our loved ones, and we feel regret. But without making mistakes, there is no way to learn. If you can learn from your mistakes, then you have already transformed garbage into flowers. Very often, our mistakes come from our unskillfulness, and not because we want to harm one another. I think of our behavior in terms of being more or less skillful rather than in terms of good and bad. If you are skillful, you can avoid making yourself suffer and the other person suffer. If there's something you want to tell the other person, then you have to say it, but do so skillfully, in a way that leads to less rather than more suffering.

## GOODWILL IS NOT ENOUGH

Your good intentions are not enough; you have to be artful. We may be filled with goodwill; we may be motivated by the desire to make the other person happy; but out of our clumsiness, we make them unhappy. Walking, eating, breathing, talking, and working are all opportunities to practice creating happiness inside you and around you. Mindful living is an art, and each of us has to train to be an artist.

## FINDING HOME

Every one of us is trying to find our true
home. Some of us are still searching. Our
true home is inside, but it's also in our loved
ones around us. When you're in a loving
relationship, you and the other person can be
a true home for each other. In Vietnamese,
the nickname for a person's life partner is "my
home." So, for example, if a man is asked,
"Where is your wife?" he might say, "My home
is now at the post office." If a guest said to
the woman, "That meal was delicious; who
cooked it?" she might answer, "My home
prepared the meal," meaning "My husband
cooked the dinner."

## OPENING THE DOOR

Once you know how to come home to yourself, then you can open your home to other
people, because you have something to
offer. The other person has to do exactly the
same thing if they are to have something to
offer you. Otherwise, they will have nothing to
share but their loneliness, sickness, and suffering. This can't help heal you at all. The other
person has to heal themselves and get warm
inside, so that they will feel better, at ease, and
can share their home with you.

## HOLY INTIMACY

Sexual intimacy can be a beautiful thing if there is mindfulness, concentration, insight, mutual understanding, and love. Otherwise it will be very destructive. When the emotional, spiritual, and physical are in harmony, then intimacy can be very holy. It is easier to practice mindful intimacy as a monk than to practice as a layperson, because it's easier to refrain from sexual activity altogether than to maintain a harmonious sexual relationship. Physical intimacy should take place only when there is mutual understanding and love.

## CHANNELING SEXUAL ENERGY

The Buddha was thirty-five, still very young, when he became enlightened. At this age we have a lot of sexual energy. It's wonderful if we can use this energy for the benefit of all beings, just as the Buddha did. The young monastics in our practice center spend a lot of time chopping wood, gardening, cooking, doing sitting meditation, and practicing walking meditation. They organize retreats, take care of their brothers and sisters, and of the friends who come from far away to spend time at our center and practice with us. They are using their energy in physical ways and living a fulfilling life. This helps them notice and be aware, without judgment, of sexual energy and learn to handle it well.

## A STRONG ASPIRATION

If you have a deep aspiration, a goal for your life, then your loving of others is part of this aspiration and not a distraction from it. If you and your partner both want to do things to relieve the suffering in this world, then your love for each other is connected to your love for others, and it expands exponentially to cover the whole world.

# WHAT LOVE NEEDS TO SURVIVE

The Buddha said that nothing survives without food, including love. If you don't know how to nourish and feed your love, it will die. If we know how to feed our love every day it will stay for a long time. One way we nourish our love is by being conscious of what we consume. Many of us think of our daily nourishment only in terms of what we eat. But in fact, there are four kinds of food that we consume every day. They are: edible food (what we put in our mouths to nourish our bodies), sensory food (what we smell, hear, taste, feel, and touch), volition (the motivation and intention that fuels us), and consciousness (this includes our individual consciousness, the collective consciousness, and our environment).

## NOURISHING OUR LOVE
## WITH EDIBLE FOOD

The first source of nourishment is edible food.
If we eat with moderation, eating only the food
we need and eating the foods that help our
bodies to be strong and healthy, then we're
showing love and respect for our bodies and
for the Earth. If we don't eat healthy foods and
don't treat our own bodies with respect, then
how can we respect other people's bodies
and the body of the Earth itself?

## SENSORY FOOD

The second source of nourishment is sensory impressions, what we consume with our eyes, ears, nose, tongue, body, and mind. When we read a magazine, we consume. When we watch a television program, we consume. Whatever we consume affects our body and mind. If we consume toxic magazine articles, movies, or video games, they will feed our craving, our anger, and our fear. If we set aside time each day to be in a peaceful environment, to walk in nature, or even just to look at a flower or the sky, then that beauty will penetrate us and feed our love and our joy.

## NOURISHING YOUR
## DEEPEST DESIRE

The third nutriment is volition. This is your desire, your hope, your aspiration. It's the energy that keeps you alive. You want to *be* someone. You want to *do* something with your life. If you're motivated by compassion and love, your volition will give you the energy and direction to grow and become even more loving and compassionate. However, if your desire is to possess or to win at all costs, this kind of volition is toxic and will not help your love to grow. You can practice developing a strong and positive volition. You can even put your commitment in words, such as: "I vow to develop understanding and compassion in me, so I can become an instrument of peace and love, to help society and the world." This kind of intention is based in our deepest aspiration.

# NOURISHING CONSCIOUSNESS

The fourth source of nourishment is collective consciousness and individual consciousness. Our individual consciousness is influenced by the collective consciousness of our environment. We absorb and reflect what is around us. If we live in a place where people are angry and violent, then eventually we'll become like them. If we live in a family or community where there's a culture of being understanding and compassionate with each other, we'll naturally be more peaceful and loving. Children growing up in such an environment will learn to be caring and kind.

# IMMEASURABLE MINDS

Loving kindness, compassion, joy, and equanimity are described as unlimited states of mind because they continue to grow and they cannot be measured. The more you practice, the more you see your love growing and growing until there is no limit. The more you practice compassion, the more it grows. The more you cultivate joy, the more joy you will feel and be able to share. The more you understand, the more you love; the more you love, the more you understand. They are two sides of one reality. The mind of love and the mind of understanding are the same.

## THE BEAUTY OF THE BODY

The human body is one of the most beautiful
things that we can see. We need to practice
treating such beauty with reverence. Perhaps
we're afraid to contemplate beauty and that's
why we don't treat our bodies and the bodies
of others with respect.

# LONELINESS AND SEX

Sometimes we think that if we have sexual relations with someone, we'll feel less alone. But the truth is that sexual relations don't relieve loneliness. There's a Vietnamese poem in which the young man has the impression that he must sit very close to his beloved to relieve his loneliness. We have the impression that if we sit close to each other we'll feel less alone. If we're separated by five meters, that's too far. Four meters is better. Three meters is still better. But even one millimeter is still too far. When our bodies are very close, we feel it will relieve this loneliness. But if we don't share our aspirations and what's in our hearts, then even if we live together or have children together, we can still feel very alone.

## DEEP LISTENING IN A COUPLE

When I meet a couple who live together and are happy, I propose that they set up a regularly structured time of deep listening to help them stay happy together. Deep listening is, most of all, the practice of being present for our loved one. We have to be truly present for the person we love. In the person we love there is suffering that we haven't seen yet. If we haven't yet understood that person, we can't be their best friend; we can't be someone who is able to understand them. It's like when an excellent musician finds someone who understands his music; they can become best friends. Someone who can understand our suffering is our best friend. We listen to each other. We are there for each other. Otherwise, the coming together of two bodies

becomes routine and monotonous after a time.
If you have the impression that you know the
other person inside and out, you are wrong.
Are you sure that you even know yourself?
Every person is a world to explore.

## FULFILLMENT

We should practice in such a way that
every moment is fulfilling. We should feel
satisfaction in every breath, in every step,
in every action. This is true fulfillment.
When you breathe in and out, there is
fulfillment. When you take a step, there is
fulfillment. When you perform any action, there
is the fulfillment that comes from living deeply
in the present moment.

## NATURAL HAPPINESS

If you walk with true awareness of every step, without having a goal to get anywhere, happiness will arise naturally. You don't need to look for happiness. When we're in touch with the wonders of life, we become aware of the many conditions of happiness that are already there, and naturally we feel happy. The beauty around us brings us back to the present moment so we can let go of the planning and worries that preoccupy us. When you look at the person you love, if he is absorbed in anxiety, you can help him get out. "Darling, do you see the sun? Do you see the signs that spring is coming?" This is mindfulness; we become aware of what is happening now and we are in touch with the conditions of happiness that are there inside us and all around us.

## MEDITATION

Meditation consists of generating three kinds of energy: mindfulness, concentration, and insight. These three energies give us the power to nourish happiness and take care of our suffering. Suffering may be there. But with the energy of mindfulness, concentration, and insight, we can embrace and take care of that suffering and nourish happiness at the same time.

## THE ART OF OFFERING HAPPINESS

In a friendship, we try to to offer our friend happiness. Sometimes you think that you're doing something for someone else's happiness, when actually your action is making them suffer. The willingness to make someone happy isn't enough. You have your own idea of happiness. But to make someone else happy, you have to understand that person's needs, suffering, and desires and not assume you know what will make them happy. Ask, "What would make you happy?"

## THE RIGHT GIFT

In Vietnam there is a fruit that many people love called durian. It has a strong smell and it's quite expensive. Many people like it very much, but I don't like it at all. Someone who sees me working very hard might think, "Oh, Thay must be very tired; I should offer him some durian." But if you forced me to eat it, I would suffer a lot. So to love someone, you have to understand the real needs of that person, and not impose on her what you think is needed for her to be happy. Understanding is the foundation of love.

# FLOWER WATERING

When we practice the art of mindful living, we water the positive elements in ourselves and each other. We see that the other person, like us, has both flowers and garbage inside, and we accept this. Our practice is to water the flower in our loved one, and not bring them more garbage. When we try to grow flowers, if they don't grow well, we don't blame them or argue with them. Our partner is a flower. If we take care of her well, she will grow beautifully. If we take care of her poorly, she will wither. To help a flower grow well, we must understand her nature. How much water and sunshine does she need?

## NO SELF

Often, when we say, "I love you" we focus mostly on the idea of the "I" who is doing the loving and less on the quality of the love that's being offered. This is because we are caught by the idea of self. We think we have a self. But there is no such thing as an individual separate self. A flower is made only of non-flower elements, such as chlorophyll, sunlight, and water. If we were to remove all the non-flower elements from the flower, there would be no flower left. A flower cannot be by herself alone. A flower can only inter-be with all of us. It's much closer to the truth. Humans are like this too. We can't exist by ourselves alone. We can only inter-be. I am made only of non-me elements, such as the Earth, the sun, parents, and ancestors. In a relationship, if you can see the nature of interbeing between you and the other person, you can see that his suffering is your own suffering, and your happiness is his own happiness. With this way of seeing, you speak and act differently. This in itself can relieve so much suffering.

## LOVE AS AN OFFERING

To love is not to possess the other person or to consume all their attention and love. To love is to offer the other person joy and a balm for their suffering. This capacity is what we have to learn to cultivate.

## THE GREATEST GIFT

One of the greatest gifts we can offer people
is to embody nonattachment and nonfear.
This is a true teaching, more precious than
money or material resources. Many of us are
very afraid, and this fear distorts our lives and
makes us unhappy. We cling to objects and to
people like a drowning person clings to a float-
ing log. Practicing to realize nondiscrimination,
to see the interconnectedness and imperma-
nence of all things, and to share this wisdom
with others, we are giving the gift of nonfear.
Everything is impermanent. This moment
passes. That person walks away. Happiness is
still possible.

## SHINING THE LIGHT

When we love someone, we should look deeply into the nature of that love. If we want to be with someone so that we can feel safe, that's understandable, but it's not true love. True love doesn't foster suffering or attachment. On the contrary, it brings well-being to ourselves and to others. True love is generated from within. For true love to be there, you need to feel complete in yourself, not needing something from outside. True love is like the sun, shining with its own light, and offering that light to everyone.

## LETTING GO OF NOTIONS

The notions and ideas we have about happiness can entrap us. We forget that they are just notions and ideas. Our idea of happiness may be the very thing that's preventing us from being happy. When we're caught in a belief that happiness should take a particular form, we fail to see the opportunities for joy that are right in front of us.

## NO SAINTS

Don't say, "Love, compassion, joy, and equanimity are the way that saints love, so since I'm not a saint, I can't possibly love that way." The Buddha was a human being, and he practiced as we do. At first, love can be tainted with attachment, possessiveness, and the desire to control. But with the practice of mindfulness, concentration, and insight, we can transform these hindrances and have a love that is spacious, all-encompassing, and marvelous.

## FRIENDSHIP

Be a friend to yourself. If you are a true friend
to yourself, you can be a true friend to a loved
one. A romantic crush is short-lived, but friendship and loving kindness can last very long
and continue to grow.

## LOOKING IN THE SAME DIRECTION

Antoine de Saint-Exupéry, the author of *The Little Prince* wrote that, "Love does not consist in gazing at each other but in looking outward in the same direction." But when two people suffer and look in the same direction, it is often the direction of the television! Over time, looking at each other and speaking with each other has become difficult and no longer brings joy. Disagreements have gone unresolved and tension and unhappiness have continued to grow. How can we bring love and happiness back into the relationship? First, we need to reflect on how we have contributed to this situation. Then we need to have the courage to turn off the television and take time to speak and listen to each other. As a true lover, the direction you look in is peace.

## A LASTING COMMITMENT

Without the pressure of other elements,
what you are now calling love may turn
sour very soon. The support of friends and
family weaves a kind of web that helps keep
a relationship strong and long-lasting. The
strength of your feelings is only one strand of
that web. Supported by many elements, your
relationship will be solid, like a tree. To be
strong, a tree sends a number of roots deep
into the soil. If a tree has only one root, it may
be blown over by the wind.

## THE ART OF CREATING HAPPINESS

What is the nature of joy and happiness? How can we touch true joy in every moment of our lives? How can we live in a way that brings a smile, the eyes of love, and happiness to everyone we encounter? Use your talent to find ways to bring happiness to yourself and others—the happiness that arises from meditation is not the same as the feeling that comes from the pursuit of pleasure seeking. Meditative joy has the capacity to nourish our mindfulness, understanding, and love. Live in a way that encourages deep happiness in your-self and others. You can vow to bring joy to one person in the morning and to help relieve the suffering of one person in the afternoon. Ask yourself, "Who can I make smile this morn-ing?" This is the art of creating happiness.

## A SLEEPING CHILD

There are times you may sit and look at a child
when she's sleeping. While the child sleeps,
she reveals tenderness, suffering, and hope.
Just contemplate a child sleeping and observe
your feelings. Understanding and compassion
will arise in you, and you will know how to take
care of that child and make her happy. The
same is true for your partner. You should have
a chance to observe him when he sleeps.
Look deeply, and see the tenderness that
is revealed, the suffering, the hope, and the
despair that can be expressed during sleep.
Sit there for fifteen minutes or half an hour and
just look. Understanding and compassion will
arise in you, and you will know how to be there
for your partner.

## LEARNING LOVE

If our parents didn't love and understand each other, how are we to know what love looks like? There aren't courses or classes in love. If the grown-ups know how to take care of each other, then the children who grow up in this environment will naturally know how to love, understand, and bring happiness to others. The most precious inheritance that parents can give their children is their own happiness. Our parents may be able to leave us money, houses, and land, but they may not be happy people. If we have happy parents, we have received the richest inheritance of all.

## FORGIVENESS

Many of us wait until it is too late to see what really matters to us. Sensual desire can feel so overwhelming that it's often not until later that we see the many important things that have needed our attention. Everybody makes mistakes, but you can't keep asking people to forgive you again and again. For example, instead of just saying, "I'm sorry I shouted at you," you can train yourself not to shout so often. Instead of a quick apology, take the time and make the commitment to practice seeing the roots of your behavior.

## 20 QUESTIONS FOR LOOKING INTO YOUR RELATIONSHIP

1   Are you in love?

2   Are you still in love?

3   Do you want to reconnect with the person who used to be the one you love?

4   Do you think that this person is happy?

5   Do you have the time for each other?

6   Have you been able to preserve your true presence for yourself and for the other person?

7   Are you capable of offering him or her freshness every day?

8   Do you know how to handle the suffering in yourself?

9   Are you able to help handle the suffering in the other person?

10  Do you understand the roots of your own suffering?

**11** Are you able to understand the suffering in the other person?

**12** Do you have the capacity to help the other person suffer less?

**13** Have you learned the way to calm down your painful feelings and emotions?

**14** Do you have the time to listen to yourself and your deepest desire?

**15** Do you have the time to listen to him or her and to help him or her suffer less?

**16** Are you capable of creating a feeling of joy for yourself?

**17** Are you capable of helping the other person to create a feeling of joy?

**18** Do you feel you have a clear spiritual path?

**19** Do you have the feeling of peace and contentment within yourself?

**20** Do you know how to nourish your love every day?

# PRACTICES FOR
# NOURISHING
# TRUE LOVE

# THE SIX MANTRAS

### ONE: I AM HERE FOR YOU

The greatest gift we can make to others is our true presence. "I am here for you" is the first of the Six Mantras. When you are concentrated, mind and body together, you produce your true presence, and anything you say is a mantra, a sacred phrase that can transform the situation. It doesn't have to be in Sanskrit or Tibetan; a mantra can be spoken in your own language. "Darling, I am here for you." If you are truly present, this mantra will produce a miracle. You become real, the other person becomes real, and life is real in that moment. You bring happiness to yourself and to the other person.

**TWO: I KNOW YOU ARE THERE, AND I AM HAPPY**

"I know you are there, and I am very happy" is the second of the Six Mantras. When I look at the full moon, I breathe in and out deeply and say, "Full moon, I know you are there, and I am very happy." I do the same with the morning star. When you contemplate a beautiful sunset, if you are really there, you will recognize and appreciate it deeply. Whenever you are truly there, you can recognize and appreciate the presence of the other, whether that is the full moon, the North Star, the magnolia flowers, or the person you love.

**THREE: I KNOW YOU ARE SUFFERING**

The third mantra is: "I know you are suffering. That is why I am here for you." When you are mindful, you will notice when the person you love suffers. If we suffer and if the person we love is not aware of our suffering, we will suffer even more. Just practice conscious breathing to produce your true presence. Then sit close to the one you love and say, "Darling, I know you suffer. That is why I am here for you." Your presence, in itself, will already relieve some of her suffering. No matter how old or young you are, you can do this.

## FOUR: I AM SUFFERING

The fourth mantra is the one you can practice when you yourself suffer: "Darling, I am suffering. Please help." There are only six words, but sometimes they can be difficult to say because of the pride in our hearts, especially if we believe that it was the person we love who caused our suffering. If it had been someone else, it wouldn't be so difficult. But because it was him, we feel deeply hurt. We want to go to our room and weep. But if we really love him, when we suffer like that, we have to ask for help. We must overcome our pride.

**FIVE: THIS IS A HAPPY MOMENT**

The fifth mantra is, "This is a happy moment." When you're with the one you love, you can pronounce this mantra. It's not autosuggestion or wishful thinking; it's waking up to the conditions of happiness that are there. Maybe you're not mindful enough, so you don't recognize them. This mantra is to remind us that we're very lucky; we have so many conditions of happiness, and if we don't enjoy them, we're not wise at all. So when you're sitting together, walking together, eating, or doing something together, breathe in mindfully and realize how lucky you are. Mindfulness makes the present moment into a wonderful moment.

## SIX: YOU ARE PARTLY RIGHT

The sixth mantra is, "You are partly right." When someone congratulates you or criticizes you, you can use this mantra. I have weakness in me and I also have strengths. If you congratulate me, I shouldn't get lost and ignore that there are negative things in me. When we see the beautiful things in the other person, we tend to ignore the things that are not so beautiful. We are human, so we have both positive and negative things in us. So when your beloved one congratulates you, and tells you that you are the very image of perfection, you say, "You are partly right. You know that I have the other things in me also." In this way, you can retain your humility. You are not a victim of illusion because you know that you're not perfect. And when another person criticizes you, you can also say, "You are partly right."

## LOVE MEDITATION

This love meditation, called Metta Meditation, is adapted from the *Visuddimagga (The Path of Purification)* by Buddhaghosa, a fifth-century C.E. systematization of the Buddha's teachings.

> May I be peaceful, happy, and light in body and spirit.
> May I be safe and free from injury.
> May I be free from anger, afflictions, fear, and anxiety.
>
> May I learn to look at myself with the eyes of understanding and love.
> May I be able to recognize and touch the seeds of joy and happiness in myself.
> May I learn to identify and see the sources of anger, craving, and delusion in myself.

May I know how to nourish the seeds of joy
in myself every day.
May I be able to live fresh, solid, and free.
May I be free from attachment and aversion,
but not be indifferent.

To begin, sit still and calm your body and your breathing. Sitting still, you aren't too preoccupied with other matters.

Begin practicing this love meditation on yourself ("May I be peaceful . . ."). Until you are able to love and take care of yourself, you can't be of much help to others. After that, practice on others ("May he/she/you/they be peaceful . . .")—first on someone you like, then on someone neutral to you, then on someone you love, and finally on someone the mere thought of whom makes you suffer. After practicing Metta Meditation, you may find you can think of them with genuine compassion.

# COMPASSIONATE LISTENING

In the practice of compassionate listening, you listen with only one purpose: to give the other person a chance to speak out and suffer less. Practice breathing in and out deeply and concentrate on what you are hearing. While the other person speaks, they may express bitterness, wrong perceptions, or make accusations. If you allow these things to touch off the anger in you, then you lose your capacity to listen deeply. Listening with mindfulness helps you to keep your compassion alive. It protects you, and your anger will not be triggered. Even fifteen minutes of listening like this can be very healing and can bring a lot of relief to another. You may be the first person who has ever listened to him or her like that.

## SELECTIVE WATERING

Selective watering is the process of watering the good seeds and giving the healthy and positive elements in our consciousness a chance to manifest. We can organize our life in such a way that the good seeds can be touched and watered several times a day.

We are the gardeners who identify, water, and cultivate the best seeds in ourselves and in others. We need some faith that there are good seeds within us, and then, with appropriate attention, we need to touch those seeds when we practice sitting meditation, walking meditation, and throughout the day. When we succeed in touching our positive seeds once, we will know how to touch them again and again, and they will strengthen.

## HUGGING MEDITATION

When we hug, our hearts connect and
we know that we are not separate beings.
Hugging with mindfulness and concentration
can bring reconciliation, healing, understanding, and much happiness. The practice of
mindful hugging has helped so many people
to reconcile with each other—fathers and sons,
mothers and daughters, friends and friends,
and so many others.

You may practice hugging meditation with
a friend, your daughter, your father, your partner, or even with a tree. Hugging is a deep
practice; you need to be totally present to do it
correctly. When I drink a glass of water, I invest
one hundred percent of myself in drinking it.
You can train yourself to live every moment of
your daily life like that.

Before hugging, stand facing each other as you follow your breathing and establish your true presence. Then open your arms and hug your loved one. During the first in-breath and out-breath, become aware that you and your beloved are both alive; with the second in-breath and out-breath, think of where you will both be three hundred years from now; and with the third in-breath and out-breath, be aware of how precious it is that you are both still alive.

When you hug this way, the other person becomes real and alive. You don't need to wait until one of you is ready to depart for a trip; you may hug right now and receive the warmth and stability of your friend in the present moment. Architects need to build airports and railway stations so that there is enough room to practice hugging. When you hug in this way, your hugging will be deeper, and so will your happiness.

## THE FIVE AWARENESSES

These verses can be practiced by anyone at anytime to help safeguard our relationships. Many people have used them in weddings and commitment ceremonies, and some couples like to say them to each other weekly. If you have a bell, you can invite it to sound after you recite each verse. Then breathe in and out a few times in silence before going on to the next verse.

1. We are aware that all generations of our ancestors and all future generations are present in us.
2. We are aware of the expectations that our ancestors, our children, and their children have of us.

3. We are aware that our joy, peace, freedom, and harmony are the joy, peace, freedom, and harmony of our ancestors, our children, and their children.

4. We are aware that understanding is the very foundation of love.

5. We are aware that blaming and arguing can never help us and only create a wider gap between us; that only understanding, trust, and love can help us change and grow.

## RELATED TITLES

Monastics and laypeople practice the art of mindful living in the tradition of Thich Nhat Hanh at retreat communities worldwide. To reach any of these communities, or for information about individuals and families joining for a practice period, please contact:

Plum Village
13 Martineau
33580 Dieulivol, France
www.plumvillage.org

Magnolia Grove Monastery
123 Towles Rd.
Batesville, MS 38606
www.magnoliagrovemonastery.org

Blue Cliff Monastery
3 Mindfulness Road
Pine Bush, NY 12566
www.bluecliffmonastery.org

Deer Park Monastery
2499 Melru Lane
Escondido, CA 92026
www.deerparkmonastery.org

*The Mindfulness Bell*, a journal of the art of mindful living in the tradition of Thich Nhat Hanh, is published three times a year by Plum Village.

To subscribe or to see the worldwide directory of Sanghas, visit www.mindfulnessbell.org.

7/15-1
8/15-2
9/15-3

6/19-16

www.parallax.org